D1276121

HowExpert Presents

Horse Care 2.0

Everything You Need to Know
About Horses for Beginners

HowExpert with
Amanda Wills

**For more tips related to this topic,
visit www.HowExpert.com/horse.**

Recommended Resources

- HowExpert.com – Quick 'How To' Guides on All Topics from A to Z by Everyday Experts.
- HowExpert.com/free – Free HowExpert Email Newsletter.
- HowExpert.com/books – HowExpert Books
- HowExpert.com/courses – HowExpert Courses
- HowExpert.com/clothing – HowExpert Clothing
- HowExpert.com/membership – HowExpert Membership Site
- HowExpert.com/affiliates – HowExpert Affiliate Program
- HowExpert.com/writers – Write About Your #1 Passion/Knowledge/Expertise & Become a HowExpert Author.
- HowExpert.com/resources – Additional HowExpert Recommended Resources
- YouTube.com/HowExpert – Subscribe to HowExpert YouTube.
- Instagram.com/HowExpert – Follow HowExpert on Instagram.
- Facebook.com/HowExpert – Follow HowExpert on Facebook.

Table of Contents

Introduction

Welcome to the world of horses. Whether you are considering your first horse, buying a new friend, or helping someone else decide whether to enter the world of equines, this is the book to read. In the following pages we will cover everything from choosing your mount to shelter, feed, and advice all beginners wish they had from others. This is not to discourage horse ownership, but to offer a realistic look into caring for, riding, owning, and dealing with some of the most common horse issues. Horses are beautiful creatures that can provide those around them with life lessons that are tough to learn anywhere else, but they are also animals that are often unaware of their size, easily scared, and sometimes unpredictable. Read on to learn and feel better prepared for your first or next experience with a horse.

Chapter 1: Choosing the Right Equine Mount for You

Choosing your first or next mount can be an exciting experience. The choices are nearly limitless when deciding on a horse. There are hundreds, possibly thousands of sites online that buy, sell, and trade horses. There are backyard breeders, trainers, traders, and individuals that will offer their horses as the best, top of the line, and green broke. There are breeds, sizes, disciplines, and so much more to consider. These will be discussed in this chapter as best as possible. It is impossible to discuss every possibility, but the most common will be covered.

When you decide to buy a horse then there are many aspects that must be considered. You need to know, realistically, what you can afford, you need to know what type of horse you want, and you should have an idea of if breed is important to you. While it may seem obvious to you in this moment, you should also account for the future as a horse is not a short term commitment. Do not be like me and luck into horse ownership. I have had many horses over the years and had the opportunity to work with and care for many that were not my own. I started as a teenager and have continued to work with, ride, and be around horses for nearly 30 years. It is always a learning process with both victories and failures, but if you are in it for the long haul, it is well worth the journey. A horse can live 30 plus years with the right care. You need to make sure you are prepared for this. These decisions must not be taken lightly as a horse, unlike a dog or cat, cannot easily be given away and cannot be taken to a kennel if you want to go on vacation. A horse is a huge commitment. When you are considering purchasing you must realize that each and every day someone must care for your horse, must feed, water, and check on the health of this large creature. This is not meant to discourage horse ownership, just a reality check that many people do not consider before making a purchase. Read on to get better insight on other and more in depth considerations about ownership.

The Best of Horse Breeds

"If you have seen nothing but the beauty of their markings and limbs, their true beauty is hidden from you."

~ Author Unknown

This writer will not pretend to tell you that there is any one or even ten best breeds of horses. There are hundreds of horse breeds and mixes (grade) horses that are not registered. In fact, my heart horse was a grade Spotted Saddle Horse that was amazing from his first ride until he was rehomed. There is no one great horse breed as each is unique. There is also no perfect horse. Each horse, even within a breed is as different as every person you meet. Each has a personality and quirks that make it different from every other. While some breeds are known for certain things, including versatility, a new owner must realize that each horse is very different, this cannot be stressed enough. This section will cover some of the more popular breeds. It will not cover all breeds as that would take volumes of books. Continue reading to get a better understanding of some of the more popular riding and driving horses in the horse realms.

Arabians are one of the oldest horse breeds and fairly common in many areas. These are highly recognizable horses as they are often compact with high tail carriage, especially when moving quickly, and a small dished nose. Hailing from the Arabian Peninsula, Arabians, are thought to be spirited horses that are great for endurance. An Arab is not often a first horse for beginners as they are typically flighty, however, they are able to be ridden and shown in all disciplines including western, saddle seat, and dressage. Most experienced people will have a strong opinion about an Arab, they will either be the only horse that should ever be ridden or too crazy to ride. The Arab is a comes in a variety of solid colors. Arabian horses were often thought of as royal horses and were first domesticated for sheiks, warriors, and even kings. Arabians were most prominent in the Middle East, but are now found worldwide in a number of disciplines. Do not let the small stature of an Arabian fool you, they are often full of energy and loyal to a single rider.

Quarter horses are a popular breed for versatility in that they can be shown in halter, barrels and everything in between. Quarter horses are an American breed that is still possibly the most popular in the United States and many are descended from a few basic bloodlines. Those familiar with Quarter horses will often recognize a name in a registered horse and be able to tell the owner what the horse was bred for as far as performance. This simply means that Quarter horses are bred specifically for certain traits. Quarter horses are known for speed over short distances, specifically the quarter mile, for which they are named. They are also well versed for other disciplines, but are typically sought for barrel racing and pole bending as their often compact bodies can easily take the turns at high speeds. However, quarter horse versatility does not stop here as they are also known for trail riding ability, jumping, western pleasure, roping, and halter classes. There are horse lines breed specifically for halter that tend to produce larger, wider horses that are well defined and some that are larger and more suited to jumping at higher levels. Just as with other breeds any horse can have a personality that does not fit its bloodlines, but someone buying a registered Quarter horse will often look at bloodlines to narrow down their search for a horse in their discipline of choice. If you are looking for an all-around horse a Quarter horse may be the perfect choice.

Thoroughbreds may be the best known breed due to the horse racing industry. Thoroughbreds began in England in the 17th and 18th centuries. It is said that Thoroughbreds can truly fly as they show more heart than most horses when matched with the right owner. In addition to racing they are often highly sought after as versatile sport horses. Thoroughbreds tend to be larger than Quarter horses or Arabs as far as height, but typically not as wide as Quarter horses. Every Thoroughbred foal is DNA tested to confirm parentage. This is a requirement for registration. Thoroughbreds are some of the fastest animals on earth, made popular by the most famous of the breed such as Secretariat and Winning Brew. If purchasing a Thoroughbred, the buyer should be aware that age is not always exact as many Thoroughbreds will be considered a year older on January 1st regardless of their actual birth date, this is to qualify for particular age groups in racing. Unless well trained or highly familiar with the breed, a Thoroughbred is not typically a first horse for individuals, however, there are exceptions to every rule.

The Tennessee Walker, a smooth gaited horse, is gaining popularity around the world. The TWH is known for its endurance and smooth gaits that make riding a comfortable experience for most. Though the TWH is best known for its smooth gait, it is still a highly versatile horse breed as many walkers can both trot and gait if trained to do so. Tennessee Walkers can be trail horses, show horses, and even jumpers and barrel racers. Though the last two are not as common, it is done. Gaited horses are capable of competing in many classes it is just not expected that they trot, but instead gait using the flat, working, and/or running walk. This gait allows for quick ground coverage. Walkers have highly varied personalities, as do most horses, but are considered a breed that works for many individuals. As someone who has ridden Walkers for many years, some are more accepting of varied jobs than others. Some do great as a laid back trail horse, while others are best suited to 'hit a big lick' in the show ring. Finding a horse with an appropriate personality for your goals is important with this breed.

The Morgan breed is not necessarily an extremely popular breed in some areas, but can be quite versatile. They are compact, like the Arbian, but considered much more agreeable overall. Considered very loyal and full of heart, the Morgan is often a choice lesson horse for beginners or young riders. Morgans are sturdy horses that carry most riders with ease as they can serve any function in or out of the show ring. If you are a taller or larger rider and wish to show then a Morgan may make you feel too tall or large for your horse. Though the horse will likely be fine to carry most riders, ascetically a larger breed may be more appropriate.

The American Paint Horse is considered a color breed as paint is not a breed as much as a combination of colors. However, paint horses do have their own registry. The most obvious characteristic is that of being dual colored over the majority of the body and built much like the Quarter horse. The often bold colors are typically what draw people to a paint horse. A registered Paint horse is a trotting breed, though spotted saddle horses do exist they are not registered by the American Paint Association. Much like the Quarter horse, a Paint can excel in a variety of disciplines and are often built much like Quarter horses.

The Appaloosa horse is also one that is highly recognizable. Appaloosa's are easily identified by their distinctive spots, a colorful coat pattern. Two distinct types of Appaloosa's are the blanket App which has a spattering of spots across the butt and the leopard App that has often loud large spots that are reminiscent of a Dalmatian dog. They are typically bold, hearty horses that are known for big bodies and sparse mane and tails. If you want a horse that you can braid, play with, and grow a gorgeous mane and tail, even though this should not be the sole purpose for owning a horse, an Appaloosa is not for you. This is characteristic of the breed and often an issue for those who wish to show. However, Appaloosas can easily be shown in numerous manners English and western, as well as trail ridden, used for barrels, poles, and much more.

Miniature horses are extremely recognizable due to their miniscule size that is under 38 inches at the withers. Miniature horses have been kept as pets by nobility, have served as show horses, and have even been used in the coal mines to move coal. Miniature horses are still often kept as pets, but do not let the small size fool you, they require the same amount of work as large horses and can be just as loving or dangerous. Even with tiny, unshod hooves, these little horses pack a punch. The challenge with miniature horses under saddle is the actual breaking as riders are often too large to actually ride the little horse. However, they can be great first mounts, though most seasoned riders would recommend a calm, larger, older horse if buying for a child.

Warmbloods, though not technically a breed, are also quite popular in many places. The Warmblood title covers several breeds. Warmbloods can range in size and look, but are typically chosen as sport or event horses. These horses are typically excellent jumpers and can be well trained in dressage as seen in many Olympic riders. Warmbloods come in a range of personalities, but are thought to be a 'hot' horse, meaning spirited and sometimes unpredictable. They may not be a great first horse for a new rider, but again, there is an exception to every rule.

The Andalusian is a Spanish breed that has been recognized for many centuries. The Andalusian was bred to be a nobility war horse that was comfortable to ride, but showed great presence in battle. The thick, flowing mane and tail are easily recognized in the breed. The most common colors for an Andalusian is grey or bay, but others do exist. Beautiful under saddle or in cart, these horses are not common in all areas, but are highly versatile.

Though not a specific breed, grade horses should also be mentioned. A grade horse is an unregistered horse and is typically a crossbreed or from parents who were not registered. This does not make a horse any less great, but it does often lower the price tag. Grade horses can be trained in any discipline and come from all breeds. Ponies are often grade and the only difference is the height. Do not be afraid to purchase an unregistered horse, they can be just as great as any horse that comes with papers. If I had to choose my perfect horse from those I owned over the years, a grade gaited horse was the one that I loved the most. While my first horse was registered, I quickly learned that it is about the horse, not the lineage.

Obviously, not every horse breed is covered here and many popular ones have been left out in the interest of being brief. The goal was just to offer an overview of some of the more popular breeds. When you are searching for your own horse do not get stuck on a specific type, color, or breed. Do not be afraid to explore your options. Specifics for each discipline will be discussed in the next section and help you move closer to finding exactly what you need.

I will close this section with a quick look into my personal horse life. My first horse was a registered Quarter Horse. I loved her and kept her until the day she died. However, she was not my heart horse. My heart horse was purchased from a horse trader many years after I had started riding. We had owned trail horses in between and I had ridden a variety of breeds, but my heart horse was a grade, two-year-old gaited gelding that I bought for a family member. He was huge and a baby and the family member would not ride him, so I took him. He was perfect in my eyes. To be honest I bought him for all the wrong reasons. I chose him because he was big, pretty, and had a gorgeous tail. This is not recommended for a first horse, but sometimes you luck into something that is perfect for you, just take your time and wait for it. That being said, I had an opportunity to buy a horse that rode perfectly for me and only me, after I found my heart horse. I rode this horse every week and was ready to buy him. He was a monster for other riders, but loved me. I took him on a trail ride, something we had done before, and he spooked. I flipped him on top of me, inches from pavement that would have killed me. I did some major bodily damage, but even after years of riding, this horse did mental and spiritual damage as well. I was broken and the mental damage took years to repair. This is just a reminder to find a horse and try it multiple times to make sure it is right for you and your situation.

The Horseback Riding Discipline that Fits Your Needs

You have taken time to read about some of the most popular horse breeds so now is the time to focus on yourself. If you have been riding for some time you probably have a feel for what you want to accomplish with horses. You have probably decided if you want to simply trail ride show, jump, do endurance, drive, or barrels. You have probably decided whether you have a preference for saddle seat, hunt seat, western, or trick riding. You may have even decided you want to do it all. If you have made this decision you are ahead of the game, but this section is for those who are not yet sure or have never really ridden and are considering horse ownership.

There is a certain appeal to buying a horse and learning with the horse. This is a commonly held thought for those who have never been around horses or who have not spent a great deal of time on horses. However, those who have had horses for years will tell you that when starting out you should get a horse that is well suited to your needs and abilities. In fact, the saying goes green (horse) + green (rider) = black and blue. Choosing a horse based on breed or how pretty you think they are in a moment is like choosing shoes because you like how they look on the shelf without checking size or price or comfort. It simply does not make sense to get a horse that you cannot ride if your purpose is to ride. On to the fun part, choosing which discipline best suits your needs.

There are four main areas of riding and showing. These include hunt seat, saddle seat, western, and driving. In each of these disciplines are a wide variety of options, but these are the main types. This is based mostly on saddles and there are other saddle options including Australian saddles, bareback saddles/pads, and side saddles. These are common, but not as common as those listed above. Your saddle in most ways determines your discipline even with the variety of events.

A western saddle is a larger saddle that has a horn. There are numerous types and styles of western saddles, but each will have a horn. The horn and the larger saddle often gives new riders a feeling of security when in the saddle as there is something to hold on to if the horse acts up. The horn is also important when roping, running cattle, and for many other purposes. Many people ride western on trails, but this is not a necessity either. When showing western pleasure, many people ride in saddles that have silver fittings and decorative scrolling. Western saddles come in all sizes, colors, and designs. Western saddles are typically leather and suede, but other materials (neoprene) are available and often cheaper. It is recommended that if showing you get a nice leather saddle, but some people prefer other materials for trail riding. Western saddles can be quite weighty so finding one that fits you, your horse, and that is easy to maneuver should be taken into consideration. It is often recommended that you find your saddle, at least a show saddle, after buying a horse as not every saddle comfortably fits every horse. There are ways to measure for a good saddle fit that may save you time and sore horses in the long run. Additionally, when showing a horse western, the rider must neck rein, meaning use one hand for horses over four years old. If just starting out it is important to find out if your horse neck reins.

Both saddle seat and hunt seat saddles are considered English forms of riding. Saddle seat riding is predominantly done on gaited horses, though Arabs and Saddlebreds, as well as others, are often ridden and shown saddle seat. A saddle seat saddle is typically leather and predominantly flat. When riding non-gaited horses, it is typical to post in this type of saddle. A hunt seat saddle is designed for both flat work and jumping. A hunt saddle does not have a horn, but has a deeper seat than a saddle seat saddle. They are typically leather, but do come made of other materials. While some people do choose to jump in other types of saddles, hunt seat saddles are designed for such activities. Hunt seat riders and saddle seat riders will ride with both hands on the reins, some horses are also shown in double bridles meaning two sets of reins.

Another common form of showing horses and just use of horses in general is that of driving. Training a horse to drive is different from teaching one to ride and while many horses can do both, if you want one that does both make sure to inquire into any training they have had. A horse will not typically just take to a new form of work, such as driving, without some basic training. Not all horses are suitable for all tasks and this is important to know and understand when making a purchase. There are numerous types of carts and harnesses and each has a different purpose in the ring or on the trail. Deciding on the type of cart is much like choosing a saddle, it must fit your purposes and your horse. Carts come in two wheeled, four wheeled, and larger versions depending on what is needed for the task you choose.

Now that you know the differences in saddles you should choose your discipline or disciplines. It is important to know what you want your horse to be able to do. One way to go about deciding what you would like to do or which style you would like to ride is to take lessons. Riding lessons are a great way to learn the basics, begin to understand what caring for a horse entails, and helping you decide on a discipline. Go on trail rides, take English and western lessons, and if possible have someone take you for a drive in a cart. Take several lessons in the style of riding you would like to attempt and try on different horses. This allows you to try different breeds and different styles so an informed decision can be made. Any experience you can have on or around horses, prior to owning one, is beneficial as you may find horse ownership is not something you really want in life. Remember, horses can live thirty years or more and you are making a commitment to them if you buy one. It is always heartbreaking to see a good, solid horse end up at a slaughterhouse simply because the owner could no longer care for its needs.

Sharing a bit of personal experience makes this real, so here goes. I bought my first horse knowing that she had received years of training as a western pleasure horse. This is what I wanted. However, my first horse was no more western pleasure than a currently racing Thoroughbred. She was not suited to the style at the time so I learned to ride hunt seat. As I became a better rider this turned into jumping. I also trail rode this horse extensively. As she got older it was hard on her joints to jump so I used her as a breeding mare and bought a gaited horse. I enjoyed English so I chose to ride both saddle seat and western. This horse did it all and it was great. Between these two horses I had the opportunity to ride and show in driving classes and even side saddle a couple times. The point is you may not want to limit yourself to one style of riding and just because your horse is trained in a particular discipline does not mean it has to stay that way or that it will do well. Keep an open mind.

Staying On Budget While Owning a Horse

If you want to make a million dollars with horses, start with a billion

~Anonymous

Buying a horse can be a big expense. As mentioned, buying a registered horse will always be more expensive. Make sure you have a budget in mind when looking at horses. It can be tempting to go with the first horse you fall in love with or when you find a good deal, but as said in the horse world, unicorns are rare. If you find a dead broke, young horse that seems too good to be true, then it probably is not real. This is especially true of those perfect horses that have a price tag of 500 dollars or less. While it is not impossible to find such animals, it is also not likely. When you are in the market for a new horse, especially a first horse, you will want to buy anything that is pretty, rideable, and the breed you want, but this may not always be the ideal situation. Just as you would take time to do research and test drive a car before buying, you should do the same for a horse. My most expensive horse was the one that not only had the highest price tag at the beginning, but continued to have health problems and get injured over time.

This is not true for all horses, but those who say you get what you pay for are not always right. Sometimes, you get what you work for and with horses, time can make a world of difference.

When you are ready to purchase a horse of your own there are some things you should consider and do long before you start looking. This section will not cover the things you need for your new horse, but just the buying process overall. The rest will be covered in other sections so make sure to read everything in each section before moving forward. First, set a budget, a range that you can comfortably afford and still pay related costs of a horse each month. While the initial purchase price of a horse is a one-time expense, there are recurring and always unexpected expenses with every horse you purchase. However, knowing and sticking to your budget for a horse is an important first step.

Now that you have a budget in mind find someone experienced with horses to help you find what you need. The word need is used instead of want because you may want a young, green broke horse, but need a beginner safe older horse. This does not mean young horses cannot be safe, but a young horse and new rider do not typically mix well. You should also be well aware of what you want to do with this horse over time. If you plan on riding daily on trails, showing, or driving, you need to know that ahead of time. Some horses do it all, some have never been off the trail and while they can be taught to show, some horses hate the show ring and will never perform well there. Figuring out what you want ahead of time through multiple lessons in different settings, different disciplines, different horses, and with different trainers is always best. This allows you to know what you want and decide on a particular breed or at least style you wish to ride or show in over time. Once you have made these decisions then you can move forward with the search.

There are numerous ways to find a horse, but each should be taken with a grain of salt. If looking online know that those who place ads are wanting to sale their horses and are not always fully honest. It is a common joke that if someone posts pictures of a child sitting on a horse that the price goes up because it is 'kid broke' or that someone standing on a horse adds several thousand to the price. Pictures lie, always visit and ride a horse in person, after the owner has ridden. Before travelling to look for a horse ask for a video, several videos of the horse being ridden in the style you have an interest in, ask about health issues, feeding schedule, and age. When you have a few prospects take time to schedule a visit. Ask that the person not have the horse ready as you will want to see whether it is difficult to catch, groom, saddle, and whether it stands to mount. Always have the owner ride first. If the owner refuses to ride, pass on the horse. Then if you are confident take a short ride. Never take your trailer on the first visit because you are more likely to end up with the horse when you will instead want to decide later, after a second or third visit. This is not because all sellers are untrustworthy, but to make sure the horse has not been medicated to make it appear calmer. This means that multiple visits should be scheduled with short notice or just by stopping by, if appropriate. There are some signs that a horse has been drugged, including a drooping lower lip, dragging feet, or even a lowered penis in geldings, but these signs are not always present and may just be signs of a relaxed horse or a medical issue. If possible, take a seasoned horse person with you to also try the horse or at least give an honest opinion.

If buying from a training barn the same applies, but you should also ask about the hours on the horse, how long they have owned, and ask to see the horse used in a lesson. You also have the option of buying from someone you know, especially if you have seen the horse used. However, know that buying from friends can end friendships if the horse does not perform well. This is not always the case, but it does happen. The key is trying the horse multiple times and being totally honest with yourself about your needs and abilities. The final steps before purchase are finding out if a buyback or return policy is in place and to get a vet check. Some issues are not noticeable at first but can be found by a vet. A buyback policy or return policy is available by some people, especially training barns, if the horse does not work out within a certain time period. Though all this work seems excessive and it can be hard to wait to get your new baby home, it is more likely that you will find the horse you need and can love for years to come.

All of the costs involved in travel, taking lessons, getting vet checks, getting any health immunizations for travel, and getting a horse delivered must be taken into account. Horse ownership is not a cheap venture and should not be taken lightly. This is not said to discourage ownership, just to help everyone find the horse best suited to their personal needs. Now that you know what to expect just in looking for a horse now we can move on to getting ready for your new best friend.

Getting Your New Horsey Best Friend

"Horses change lives. They give our young people confidence and self-esteem.

They provide peace and tranquility to troubled souls. They give us hope!"

~ Toni Robinson

Simply saying that a horse can change your life is an understatement. Having a horse be part of your life can create a bond that is unbreakable. When you find your heart horse you will want to do anything and everything with and for that horse that is possible. You will cherish every moment that you get to spend with this magnificent beast and together you will feel like you can take over the world. A horse can become a best friend and a confidant when it works and can become a danger when it doesn't. If you have found a horse that works for you, congratulations. You are ready to bring your new best friend home. I have spent many hours talking to my horses and crying into their soft coats. Your horse can save you from yourself simply because they need you, if you are willing to take on that responsibility. This can sometimes be a challenge and creating a safe place is important. Specifics are discussed in further sections, but an overview will be offered here. You need to have a safe place to house your horse. While some are content to be pasture kept, they still need a safe place to get out of the weather, sound fencing, and an area free from anything that could be harmful to eat. You should also have feed and hay ready for your new mount.

Additionally, you should know whether the horse has been on pasture and if not then limited grass will have to be introduced slowly over a few weeks.

If your horse needs to be brought to you there will be an additional cost for transport and any health certifications necessary for travel must be arranged. This usually means at the least, a Coggins and immunization record. While immunizations are not a necessity in all states, if the horse crosses state lines then it is a requirement. If you have a hauler bringing the horse than make sure they have the proper insurance in case of an accident. You should also prepare a fresh source of water for your horse and have at least a halter and lead available immediately. It can take a few days for your horse to explore and adjust to a new environment so keep a close eye on your new friend.

If your horse is to be taken to a boarding stable make sure the stable will hold a place for your horse and that they have a quarantine area available. Even a perfectly healthy horse coming into a new barn could potentially get sick or get others sick since they are moving from a different barn. Quarantine should last a minimum of ten days before other animals are allowed around the new horse. This time also allows for you to observe your horse's habits, likes and dislikes, and bathroom habits as many things can be learned from these simple observations. Quarantine is also a wonderful time to spend quiet moments with your horse simply grooming, doing ground work, and creating a stronger bond. Read on to learn what you definitely need and possibly want before your horse arrives.

Chapter 2: Helping Prepare for your Horse

You have found a horse you like and it is possibly arriving very soon. It is time to get ready! This section will discuss the basics sans food and hay that will be covered in other sections. This is more about the everyday items that can be used over and over, halters, leads, buckets, etc. Depending on the time of year you purchase your horse and where you live, the needs may be slightly different. While it is often cheaper to buy a horse in colder months it can also be more expensive to offer care at that time of year. So to prepare, take all of this into account.

Meeting Basic Horse Needs

There are some basics you will need before your horse arrives. In fact, these few things should be in place before your first horse ever comes home. This section will not cover shelters as that is a whole other topic, but will cover the few must haves before your new friend comes home or heads to a boarding facility. The most important things you can have for your new horse are a lead rope and a couple well-fitting halters. While this may not seem like much these two items will make your life much easier. You can often find out halter size from previous owners or make a strong guess based on your horse's size. The type of halter you use is also important. If your horse is to be turned out in a halter, which is not recommended but is often necessary for a few days, a breakaway halter is important. This allows the horse to get free if they are trapped by the halter. A horse kept in the stall will not need haltered full time, but this is still needed for moving around a barn or property. A leather halter is typically very strong but will need cleaned often. A nylon halter or any halter you can get from a farm store is usually washable and can be easily replaced and holes added if needed. Rope halters are also good products and easily adjustable if you know the proper tying technique. Do not assume your new horse will come with a halter or lead as this is not always the case. Having at least two halters assures that if one if lost or broken, a replacement is readily available. This is also true of lead lines. Get one that is long enough for tying and strong enough to stand up to a horse. Have extra leads to use for cross tying and in case of a broken rope. When buying a lead rope, a strong, braided or twisted rope is best and less likely to break. Make sure the hook/buckle is also heavy duty in case the horse pulls when tied or being led.

Depending on your horse, and what you need, a few brushes are also necessary. You want to be able to bond with your new friend over grooming and groundwork so it is always handy to have a stiff brush, shedding blade, and face brush available. It also comes in handy to have a tangle free brush for the mane and tail. Extras such as smaller brushes, sponges, and any small item you may want can wait, but the basics, are well, the basics.

If your horse is coming to your home and in many cases if they are going to a boarding facility, a basic first aid kit is also important. This should include at minimum gauze, vet wrap, antibiotic ointment, a thermometer, some sanitary pads which are great for packing a wound or wrapping a leg, some blood stop, a needle and syringe, and possibly some Bute or other pain medication if available. You will also want some form of fly control if insects are an issue at that time of year.

There are numerous extras that may be needed or wanted and these will be covered a little further in the text. However, these are the very first things to invest in as horses require lots of little things in their first days. As someone who has owned horses for many years I can honestly say I have spent millions. I am not rich, but stuff tends to accumulate.

Providing Feed and Hay for Your Horses

The key things you need to have for your new horse are two to four buckets, one for feed and one for water and at least one extra just in case. If you live in extremely cold climates then a heated bucket is a great investment, but they do require electricity to keep ice from forming. If you are choosing to use a large tub for water, like in a field, then rubber does not freeze as quickly as metal, but can be more difficult to keep clean. Either tub type can be used with a tank heater that also requires electricity. It is highly important that your horse has access to clean water at all times. If your tank does get dirty there are many ways to prevent bacteria and algae growth and a good weekly cleaning with vinegar and a tiny bit of bleach is also highly recommended. Keep the water in shade if possible to encourage drinking in the hotter months. While buckets can be used to feed there are also specialized feeders that are wider as well as rubber pans that offer ease of access. These should also be cleaned often. Can you imagine if you had to eat off of a dirty plate each day?

Hay is also an issue as some horses do fine with free feeding from a round bale in a field, while stall kept horses will need access to hay daily. This can be placed in a hay bag, in a corner holder, or on the ground. Though ground placement often leads to wasted hay over time. There are round bale feeders available and patterns available to build one yourself.

The amount of hay and feed your horse requires will depend on their physical condition and what they are used to having. An overweight horse may require less grain, but will still need hay. Hay and forage is important for a horse's overall health as it helps with digestion. An underweight horse will require more grain, but this must be done slowly as overfeeding can result in health issues that are irreversible or even deadly. You may have to start with the type of grain the horse was used to at the previous owner as some are picky eaters and slowly switch to a feed of your choice. Some owners will send feed with a horse to help with the transition, so feel free to inquire ahead of time.

Be aware that some horses will not transition well and may refuse to drink or eat for a day or two. As long as they are in good health just keep offering small amounts of feed and keep an eye on your new friend. Make sure they have easy and safe access to salt and/or mineral blocks as this encourages health and drinking, as well as providing necessary supplements. Treats are safe for most horses, but make sure not to go overboard. Many horses do not have a shut off switch and will eat continually, enough to make themselves sick, if allowed to do so. Make sure all feed and treats are stored safely in an area away from the animals and any insects or other creatures that could ruin the feed. Metal trash cans, feed boxes, and even old freezers are great storage options. This way mice cannot chew through plastics and contaminate feed. While hay storage away from mice is not always a possibility it is necessary to store your hay in a dry place when not in use. Some people store hay in the barn while others have a separate storage area that will be discussed in the barn and storage section. Make sure creatures such as opossums and raccoons are kept away from hay as these can carry diseases that cause great harm to horses.

Though the access to water has been touched upon it is an important topic. Horses need lots of water each day, in the hottest month your horse could drink 20 gallons or more every day. Water should be kept in a place where it does not get too hot, but offers easy access. Tanks also tend to get dirty faster in direct sunshine during the summer months, but cleaning is simple with a brush and diluted bleach. Many people also use a cup full of apple cider vinegar in a large tank to cut down on bacterial growth.

Preparing a safe area for your horse to eat, drink, and get exercise is just the beginning of meeting the needs of your new best friend. As is keeping these areas clean and free from anything dangerous. Keep reading for ways to stay on budget for the little extras you may want or need as a new horse owner.

Having Fun with Horse Extras without Going Overboard

The horse world offers an easy opportunity to go broke. Horses do have certain needs, but there are thousands or extras that have been created to appeal to the horse lover in us all. If you want a bridle that has been blinged out with crystals, they can be found, a saddle that is more silver than leather, piece of cake. Whether you want a tack room filled from top to bottom with stuff or simply a box with a few extra brushes, the horse world will accommodate. In this section we will review some of the extras that you will actually use in showing, trail riding, and storage. Many items are perfectly fine to buy used and others have to be bought new to still be useful. Read on to learn of some of the useful products that you will likely need over time. Please know that not all horses will need these items and all can survive without them, but they can make life easier overall.

If you are going to ride you will need a good saddle, quality bridle, and a saddle pad. The type and style of saddle will depend on your discipline and the price range can vary widely. Make sure you get a saddle that properly fits your horse so no sores will develop. Kits are available to measure saddle size to properly fit withers and back. Try out several saddles in a variety of brands to find the perfect fit for you as well. Make sure you choose a saddle you are comfortable in and with stirrups that can be easily adjusted to fit your leg length. You will have a choice of girth types as well and should make sure your girth can be adjusted to fit your horse if they gain or lose weight and one that does not rub or otherwise bother your new friend.

Your bridle will also depend on the discipline you choose. Simple trail bridles are available as are cheaper leather versions in both English and western. Your bridle should fit without gaps, yet should not be so tight that it does not give. When choosing a saddle and bridle it is always helpful to have a knowledgeable person go with you to shop. Many products can be found online, but check return policies as they may be of poor quality or not fit upon arrival. When choosing a saddle pad make sure to get one that is full enough to offer protection for your horse, that is fitted to your saddle, and that is appropriate for the discipline you choose. If you show or ride in more than one discipline you are likely to need multiple saddles, bridles, and saddle pads as well as appropriate show clothes. When first starting it is best to buy used clothing as you may change your mind later. The one thing you should not buy used is a well fitting helmet. While there is a forever, on-going debate over wearing a helmet when riding, it is the safest option. Get properly fitted for a helmet if you do choose to wear one.

Once the basic riding gear is acquired you will need some extras for your horse. There are numerous types of saddle bags, saddle covers, horse boots, polo wraps, blankets, brushes, buckets, fly masks, and much, much more. While having extra brushes, halters, and lead ropes is always good, they are not something you need to buy immediately. A blanket may be a necessity if your horse is used to wearing one. These come in many forms and patterns with fly sheets being the lightest. Some are water proof, some are lined, and most all are washable. Some blankets and sheets are stretchy, while some hook on using Velcro, snaps, or buckles. Blankets must be measured to fit appropriately. The way to measure a blanket for your horse can be found online with just a few keystrokes. When buying a blanket do not assume that sizes are standard as different brands can vary greatly. Fly masks are optional and many horses have the amazing ability to get them off in a matter of minutes. Some horses may not even wear one as they do not like things on their face. Products for shipping such as polo boots or wraps are also available for horses. Not everyone uses these products, but they can be a safety product for long trips and can also come in handy for horses with white legs when going to a show. If you choose to use polo wraps or boots make sure to learn how to properly wrap legs so the horse is not injured or circulation accidently hindered.

The number of brushes and grooming supplies that are available for a horse could fill several novels. There are stiff brushes, hair brushes, shedding blades, sweat scrapers, sponges, banding kits, braiding kits, and so much more. You do not need a million brushes, but having extras over time does come in handy. A stiff brush is perfect for the body and upper legs, while a soft brush is ideal for the face. A brush with medium stiffness is best for those with sensitive legs. You will need a hoof pick to make sure your horse's feet stay debris free. During shedding season, a shedding blade or curry comb is a life saver as hair collects in bristled brushes and can be hard to remove. If you are working your horse into a sweat often or plan on bathing, a sweat scraper will help you get excessive moisture off your horse.

In addition to grooming supplies you will need extras such as shampoo, conditioner, soap, and first aid supplies. The shampoo and conditioner can be for human use though stuff with a strong floral or fruit smell often attracts bugs. If you choose not to use shampoo, then Dawn dishwashing liquid works well for baths and gets the white on your horse extremely white. You will need a stocked first aid kit that can be built over time but should include the things listed above as well as extra needles and syringes, penicillin (refrigerated), extra vet wrap and gauze, fly spray, alcohol, and iodine. These are the basics and at times you may need further supplies, but this is the stuff you are most likely to use. Additionally, you will need to buy leather cleaner for your saddles and bridles, and cheap, scent free detergent to wash blankets and halters in when needed. Some people choose to use vinegar to wash tack and blankets to remove smells, but it does not always function to clean as well. The final must have for both health and if showing are a good set of clippers. Clippers can be a pricey item. Make sure you read reviews, compare prices, and get opinions from those you know when buying clippers. These are items that will hopefully last a few years so do not fear paying a little extra for a great pair. For quick stray hair clipping, a small battery operated pair is perfect, but for show clipping of bridle paths, legs, etc. a full size pair with extra blades will be necessary. These are not things you need immediately, but should be gathered over the first couple months of horse ownership.

Must haves for a barn will be covered in a different section, but there are other products you may need to ride. The first, if you have trouble mounting is a sturdy step ladder or a mounting block. These can be bought or built very easily. You may also want to invest in a round bale feeder at some point and even a round pen. These can be bought used and function well for many years. You may want to keep extra buckets and feed pans available as well, in case something breaks or gets damaged. Finally, at some point you may want to purchase a horse trailer. This will require a vehicle that can carry not only the weight of the trailer, but the weight of a horse. Horse trailer sizes, types, and varieties are numerous and time for research should be taken before purchase.

Again, there are millions of things, toys, treats, and decorations you can purchase for your new horse. As time goes on you will probably splurge and do just that, but do not go overboard right away. Take time to get to know your horse, your needs, and your wants. There may be some items you need sooner than others and some you can hold off on or purchase used. Horses are big commitments, not just in the initial purchase, but over time. This book is designed to remind people of that and help them prepare ahead of time so both the owner and horse are safe and happy. I may not be the best representation of this section as I own or have owned halters of every type and color, been known to buy a saddle on a whim, and have horse products that have never been used. Have fun, but try to keep your needs separate from your wants over time.

Chapter 3: Building the Ideal Horse Shelter

Horses need shelter. It is a strange fact that horses will spend more time outdoors in cooler temperatures, if given the option, but horses do need some form of shelter throughout the year. While many horses are pasture kept, they still need an area that is covered and safe. There are numerous types of horse barns and shelters that can be created. A few of the most common will be shared and described below, as well as specific aspects of a barn that may be beneficial when owning horses.

Creating a Horse Barn

If you are lucky enough to own a horse and be able to keep it on your property, then you will need some type of shelter. Even horses that are predominantly kept in a pasture will need some sort of shelter in that pasture or to return to if poor weather or excessively hot weather occurs. Having a shelter or barn is also a safety issue as an injured horse will need a place to stay for a few days if needed. As mentioned there are hundreds of barn types and the designs found within those barns and shelters are unlimited. A few aspects of shelters and barns will be shared here with some cost effective options if you are building from the ground up. I was lucky enough to help design my own barn and have it custom built on our property. I thought I knew exactly what I wanted, but even your best barn will end up having things you wish you could change. The goal is to keep your horse happy and be willing to admit that nothing is ever perfect, but you can work with it. Enjoy your horse and your space, that is what truly matters.

For horses that are pasture kept you may not want to start by building a large barn. Most horses that do not need to be stalled for any length of time are fine with a covering that allows them to get out of bad storms or excessive heat. It often surprises new owners to see their animals standing out in a spring shower or during a heavy snow fall, but the horses do not necessarily feel cold in the same way, the shelter is much more important for heat relief. A lean to type shelter with three sides and a roof is perfect for a single horse. These can be put together very easily in a day or two and are highly cost effective. Additionally, a gate can be added to the front and a divider if stalls ever need to be created or the horse kept stationary for a period of time. Most of these shelters are made of wood and a simple metal tube gate can be used to contain the horse. A lean to is also a great place to keep the water tub if the shelter is big enough for the horse to lie down, roll, and stand comfortably with the tub also in there. This will keep debris out of the tank and keep the water cooler overall. It is probably obvious, but if you have more than one horse than the size of the lean to or a second lean to should be added to allow for shelter.

Another option for those who prefer not to self-build is a carport. The large metal carports are big enough for horses to walk through and offer shelter from the elements. These can be purchased new or used in a variety of sizes. As these are quite bulky you must make sure you have room to place such a structure and if possible have one with at least two sides filled in to offer a break from the wind for your horses. A three sided carport would also work, but may become overly hot in warmer months as the metal will hold in the heat. If cost is a concern an open carport with just a roof can have tarps added to the sides to block weather as needed. If using a carport, make sure it is well grounded with the base weighted so strong winds do not tip it over and create a safety issue. The only downfall to a carport is the difficulty one can have dividing it into stalls if no sides are present, but it is possible with a little creativity. Any lean to or carport that is used as shelter should be tall enough for your horse to have plenty of leg and head room. A minimum of seven to eight feet tall is preferable. Larger shelters such as those just described are also a great place to put daily hay rations or place round bales to keep from the hay getting wet and wasted.

If you are going full speed into horse ownership, it is likely that your tiny herd of one will turn into two very quickly. This is not only because horses are herd animals and need a friend, but because horses are addictive. Perhaps you will start with a single horse and a goat or some chickens, but at some point the majority horse owners make the leap to owning a second horse, especially if those horses are kept at home. If you have a single or multiple horses or if you plan on showing, it is best to have a barn that offers individual stalls. Stalls allow for each horse to have their own space which makes health monitoring easier. Stalls also mean a well bedded, safe, and clean space for horses to wait after a bath or in preparation for a show.

If there is a barn on your property, consider yourself lucky. Most barns can easily be altered to accommodate horses. You should make sure that any already built barn has space for stalls, an area to tie horses, and if possible an area to store feed and tack. The building needs to have plenty of head room for horses and footing that does not hold moisture. Dirt floors are common and are fine as long as water does not pool and create constant mud as this is bad for feet. Concrete floors in a walkway are easy to clean and offer sure footing as well. Some people also have concrete stalls, but as this can be damaging to a horse's feet a thick layer of bedding will be needed. Many choose to use sawdust or straw over dirt or pea gravel flooring to keep moisture to a minimum. Another option is the use of stall mats; most mats are placed over small gravel that also rests on a dirt floor. It is important to keep your mats covered with bedding and occasionally spray off the tops of mats and allow for air drying. The ammonia from horse urine can create strong smells and create an unhealthy environment if not removed often. Horses allowed to stand in wet conditions, especially in urine, can develop a condition called thrush that can cause great damage to the feet.

If the barn has an area to store tack it should be well sealed to keep moisture from ruining leather or creatures coming in that can damage tack. Mice will chew on saddles, bridles, and any feed that is left exposed. Many barns also have hay storage beside or above the stalls. Hay storage above the stalls in a hay loft can make moving hay difficult and is thought by many to be dangerous in case of a fire as hay can ignite very quickly. Hay stored in a separate building or in a separate part of the barn may be safer, but should still provide easy access for feeding. A barn without stalls is still usable for horses as stalls can be built or the building itself can be used as a run-in, especially for a single horse or even a pair of horses.

For those of us that have to create or want to create a barn from the ground up there are many things to consider. First, you will want to choose your size and types of material. Many barns are made of predominantly wood, though metal buildings are gaining fast popularity. Regardless of the material chosen, you have other choices that have to be made. It is always ideal to have extra stalls while still keeping within your budget. Even if you only have one horse you should have at least two or three stalls. The extra stalls can be used for storage of feed, tack, and other items that can cause clutter in a barn. Eventually, most horse lovers will fill those stalls with more horses, but the extra space always comes in handy even if extra horses are never acquired. In choosing stall types you should consider your horse's needs and what you want to do now and in the future. Tie in stalls are an option if you do not plan to leave the horse in for long periods of time. Tie in stalls usually have the horse with its backside toward a center walkway and is fine for short term tying. Stalls can also be created with gates or spaced boards which works for many horses, however, there is a risk of a horse putting a foot through the spaces or rolling and getting caught which can cause major damage to both the animal and the barn. Another option are enclosed stalls with doors that either open out or slide. These fully enclosed stalls should give the horse the option to lie down, roll, and move around. While horses do stand most of the time, many like to lie down to relax. In fact, it is pretty common for a horse to lie down immediately upon fresh bedding being put into a stall. Stalls should be kept clean and well bedded so your horse is comfortable while they stand for any amount of time. If using enclosed stalls make sure hay, feed, and water buckets or holders are well secured. If your horse is going to be in the stall throughout the day or night or both, placing a salt or mineral block holder is always a good idea.

Now that you have an idea forming about the type, style, and form your barn should take, let's look at the extras that can be added to a barn. Extra stalls for storage have been mentioned, but a separate tack room can come in handy. This is a room for tack and extra horse supplies, which will accumulate quickly. Having an area with hooks or a peg board that can be readjusted as needed is great for hanging bridles, halters, and lead ropes. Saddle stands are also important. Moveable saddle stands can be purchased as can those that have multiple tiers which are always handy. Additionally, saddle stands can be easily built with wood blocks and hinges. This type stand can be raised to hold the saddle and lowered when not in use. These are perfect for in the tack room and even in the barn as a place to leave a saddle while grooming. If electricity and water are readily available in a barn a small dorm size refrigerator for barn supplies comes in useful and an electric fence conductor can be safely placed inside and out of the weather. A small refrigerator is perfect for holding any medications that need to remain chilled and adds a place to hold treats and even drinks for riders and guests. If necessary, a tack room can also hold feed away from the tack in metal cans or an old freezer that is left unplugged. Some people use plastic containers, but as mice and other creatures are often attracted to the feed it is best if plastic is not used. A final idea for a tack room is to have built in shelving with removable containers for brushes or a table to use to clean tack as needed and place buckets with brushes and supplies on when not in use.

Assuming you are creating your dream barn you could create a separate feed room. This would be a room with a separate door and feed safe containers. There should also be a space for any supplements that are being fed, as well as treats. A separate feed room would not have to be large, but would allow for extra storage of the many feed items that will accumulate over time. This area will also come in handy if you have multiple horses with different feeding needs. If using removable feed pans or over the fence feeders this is also a safe storage area in which each can stay.

Another extra for barn builders is a separate area for hay. If you are a horse owner it is usually best to accumulate enough hay for winter during the summer months when it is cut. For a winter season that lasts on average four months, when hay is often costlier and harder to find, it takes about 100 large square bales per horse. This is assuming a single bale lasts a day or two. This can vary greatly. If you are feeding from a round bale, expect to store about ten round bales for the fall/winter months before the grass starts growing well again. This is just an average and will vary greatly from horse to horse and based on bale size. Some people choose to buy hay a couple round bales or squares at a time and if a supplier is readily available, this is fine, but having extra is always beneficial. If you build a separate hay area, make sure it is easily accessible from the barn in all weather conditions. You will also want to make sure the hay is off the ground and remains dry at all times. Wood pallets are a great way to get the bottom bales off the ground. While tarps will probably keep hay dry, tears can occur. Moldy hay cannot be fed to horses as it can cause colic, among other health issues.

The actual design of your barn will also vary. Some people choose to have a center walkway in a long barn with all doors opening toward that walkway on either side. Some will choose to have stalls along the outside so horses can look out with an overhang to prevent rain from falling in the stalls. Some have round barns; some have stalls along two walkways. Recently, barns have also been designed with extra areas so each horse can have a round bale placed outside each stall in a dry area and the horses are allowed to eat at will. If you can dream it, your barn can be created in that way. When creating your barn, visit others. Talk to people to see what they like and what they wish they had done differently to see what works for you.

Finally, there are more extras to consider for your barn. A must have is a place or places to tie your horse. D-rings on either side of a walkway or main doorway is a perfect spot for crossties. If crossties are not an option, then the same D-rings can be used for single line tying. An optional addition that can be completed later on is a wash rack. This is usually a large partially enclosed cement block with a drain or at a slight angle that allows for bathing in case of injury or preparing for a show. While a barn is fully functional without such an area it is highly useful. A couple other options that are not directly connected to the barn are a round pen, a small pen used for lunging and training and/or an arena. If you are going to predominantly trail ride, these may not be necessary, but they are useful for all horse owners.

So far, shelters and personally designed barns have been discussed. There is another option. Companies have now started creating standard and made to order barn shells that can be configured to your personal needs. These shells are purchased and the company can be paid to install them on your property. Additionally, premade stalls can be installed, built in your barn in the style you want. Depending on your barn size this may be a cost effective option. These barns are available worldwide from different companies. So if designing your own barn seems overwhelming, take a look at their options and configurations to find one that works for you.

Types of Horse Boarding Options

Until now this text has assumed that you would keep your new equine friend at home, but many owners and riders choose to board. There are a number of reasons people may choose to board instead of keep a horse at home, but time, space, and need of a trainer are the top reasons. Many horse owners simply do not have the time or space for a new horse. While this may not be ideal for some, it is a perfect compromise for others. Some people choose to board temporarily while they prepare their own property, while others board for the entirety of their riding career. Boarding offers the opportunity to have someone else care for your horse if an issue arises and you cannot for short period. This is perfect for those that work unpredictable hours or who may need to travel and would not have a trained person to look after their horsey friend. Boarding may also allow access to the trainer of your choice, which is highly beneficial for beginners. In fact, most seasoned horse people would recommend many lessons with a trainer before ever purchasing a horse. Additionally, spending time helping out or working in a boarding stable will give you an idea of the care needed for a horse long before purchase. Some stables will even allow the trading of work and chores for lessons. This is a free or cheaper way to earn some saddle time even if you do not own a horse.

If you are going to board at a barn it is important to check out the barn in person more than once. Make an appointment if needed the first time, but if possible unscheduled visits are always a great way to see how the barn is truly run. Make sure your potential boarding situation has good access to water for your horse, has safe pasture area, and that the type of boarding you want and need is available. Feel free to compare prices and amenities for several boarding stables as each will be different. Find out what is expected of you as an owner. Questions about being able to use your own farrier or vet should be asked, as well as information about what type of insurance the boarding stable carries. All boarding stables are legally required to carry insurance in case you are injured, your horse is injured, or your horse injures someone else. This is non-negotiable for boarding stables. When choosing a stable, you should also inquire into barn rules and the contract that is signed by boarders. Contracts are to keep you and your horse safe and for you to be made aware of what happens in given situations, such as emergencies or late payments.

I boarded for many years. I started boarding with the lady I took lessons from when learning to ride. I followed her to several boarding stables over time before finally being able to bring my horses home. I learned that you must decide whether you like the barn, the trainer, or the people. You may need to be willing to leave to follow a trainer or friends, so choose wisely. We were in five different barns in over fifteen years, some because the stables closed and a few because it was not a great situation. Be prepared for the unexpected with horses.

If you do choose to board, know that there are a number of types of boarding available and not all may fit what you want or need. Some barns offer pasture or stall board, while some offer both. Pasture board only means your horse will not have a stall and will be left in a field, probably with other horses, at all times. Many of these situations mean that your horse will not have a readily available stall if needed. Most pasture boards will also do field feeding with the use of a round bale. However, some will bring horses in daily just to eat and leave a round bale in the field. If you do primarily field or pasture board, make sure fresh clean water is always available and shelter to house the number of horses in the field is safe and available. As with any boarding situation, check fencing. Anything with a barbed wire fence should probably be avoided as this is dangerous for horses. Make sure any wooden or plastic fences are in good repair and any wire type fencing is well marked. Most horse boarding situations will also have at least one strand of electric to keep horses from breaking through the fencing when playing or if spooked.

Many that board have both stall and pasture available. This means your horse has a stall, but daily or multiple turn outs a week are possible. Turnout may be dependent on weather or other factors such as number of horses. You may also have the option of day or night turnout which is great for darker horses that can bleach in the sun. In addition to the type of housing your horse will have, you will also want to take your riding needs into consideration. You should look for a riding arena with solid grounding, an indoor arena if your area is prone to poor weather, and access to trail rides if that is your main goal. Many stables will also offer access to their trainers. Sometimes this is included in board, other times lessons are considered extra. Some higher end barns will also offer extras such as a trainer working with your horse at various tasks to being able to call ahead and your horse being groomed and ready to be ridden when you arrive. Different barns definitely offer various services, but everything comes at a price. Your needs will determine what works best in your budget and for your purposes.

Another aspect of stable or barn boarding that should be considered is what is included. Some stables offer just a place for your horse to stay and you are required to provide feed, hay, and basic care. Other barns, much more common, offer a stall or pasture board, hay, and feed that is given a set number of times and cleaning of stalls. Any supplements, treats, or extras you may want or need will come from you or be an added expense. Most times if supplements are needed you can purchase the extras and the barn hands will add it to feed. This should be determined prior to choosing a stable for your horse. You may also want to ask about vet and farrier care for that barn and hours that the barn is open for use. Many stables have extensive hours, but some will limit the hours you can actually use the facility. Make sure to choose a space that works with your schedule.

If you choose a barn with a live in or daily trainer there is a chance that board will be higher and you will be expected to ride or take lessons a set amount of times. This can make you a better, well versed rider over time, but may overwhelm others. You should also meet fellow boarders to make sure this is a place you will enjoy coming over time. Your horse can quickly become your new best friend, your heart, and your confidant, so choose those people you can be around while you enjoy this time. Additionally, find out rules about bringing others to the barn to ride your horse or just to visit as this is not always allowed or welcomed at some stables.

A final couple pieces of advice may sound repetitive, but are important enough to address again. First, take lessons and possibly lease a horse before buying your own. Lesson horses are so accustomed to many riders they are used to everything and do not give you a true feeling of what it is like to own a horse. Second, and most importantly, go see your horse daily or in the least, several times a week. This way you will learn your horse's habits and routines and will quickly recognize if a problem has started or has gotten worse. Finally, when choosing a boarding stable, choose wisely. Some stables are very breed specific and will look down upon or not accept other breeds. Some show barns will look down upon grade horses or those who do not wish to show. Choose a barn that works for the type of riding and skill level you wish to achieve as this can vary greatly. The key is to feel comfortable at your barn as you will be visiting very often and it should feel like a second home.

Chapter 4: Knowing the True Cost of Horse Ownership

If you are still reading to this point and still want a horse of your own, then you are lucky. So many people rush into horse ownership with no clue of how much time, energy, and money is needed. There are ways to cut costs, but for the most part these are accident prone creatures that can rack up vet bills very quickly. You may be lucky and never have a horrible accident with a horse, but chances are if you stick with riding you will have to make a vet call, lost shoe call, or an 'I need a trainer' call at some point. Continue reading to know when those calls should be made and how to find someone who will work for and with you and your horse.

Knowing your Equine Vet (and when to Call)

Prior to buying your first horse or even when you are moving to a new area with a horse, you need to look into large animal vets. It is preferable to have two large animal vets that you can call. You should also find out if they are mobile, can come to your horse, or if hauling is necessary. The need for two is in case of an emergency when one is out of town or unable to get to your horse in a timely manner. Call the vet's office ahead of time and see what their policies are on making farm calls, check on basic fees, and emergency fees, as well as how to make contact in case of an emergency. It is important to know these things both for yourself and your horse ahead of time. If you are boarding, it is likely that a barn vet is on call and some stables require you to use their vet, but if you must choose your own, choose wisely.

There are many times your vet will be necessary and many times when you can take care of your own horse issues. Horses will get hurt. It is inevitable. The moment you feel your horse is totally safe, is the moment your horse will find a creative way to injure itself. This is not to discourage horse ownership, but to provide an honest picture of what it will be like in the long run. Horses will trip and come up lame, they will eat things that make them sick, they will even run into sticks, posts, and fences that they have seen a million times before. Those who have been in the horse world for years will tell you that putting your horse in a bubble wrapped stall will not make a difference, they can still get injured. It should also be noted that the smaller the horse, the more likely they will squeeze into or out of an area that they were not supposed to be in or escape from. Horses are wonderful, beautiful animals that can get into some interesting situations. Take a look at Google images and type in horses in weird situations, you will find pictures of horses stuck between gates, climbing hay bales, stuck in holes, and so much more. While those pictures are funny and all too familiar to seasoned horse owners, they are also the start of some pretty impressive injuries.

Basic injuries and even some basic horse vet care can be handled at home by you. However, if you have not been taught proper procedures such as how to wrap a leg, how to treat sore feet, how to treat an abscess, or how to give a shot then ask for help from someone who has experience. This means that an older horse person or a vet may need to teach you these skills the first time, but you will learn to handle the minor issues in time. A great way to learn prior to owning a horse is to volunteer at a stable or large animal vet, this way you have someone with experience and you can learn new skills. Working with large animals is much different than small animals, especially in how badly you can be injured or how much damage can be done if something is treated incorrectly. Though horses are large animals, they are surprisingly fragile in many ways. Some of the more common horse issues and treatments, as well as, when to call for help are included in this section.

Horses are large animals that are typically kept outdoors for a good portion of their life, so skin conditions are relatively common. There are some that are more common than others. These include Ringworm, Rain scald, Mud Fever, Cracked heels, and Sweet itch. Each of these conditions are treatable and can be treated by the owner with basic methods, especially if caught early. Even though some can be owner treated, antibiotics or special sprays may need a vet prescription to obtain.

Ringworm is common in horses and is contagious to humans through both direct and indirect contact. This means it is important to keep brushes and tack clean and not share with other horses that may be contagious. Infected horses should be isolated when possible and this includes outside turnout. Proper hygiene methods must be practiced in all areas this horse is staying or standing as the bedding, ground, and all items that touch that horse can spread ringworm. To clean brushes and to disinfect stalls, antifungal spray and wipes need to be used throughout and after treatment. All used bedding should be completely stripped out daily to minimize treatment time. If safe, it is also advisable to burn the bedding. The person cleaning should also make sure to spray cleaning items and even shoes to prevent the spread of the fungus. Those horses with ringworm will begin showing with raised, often round, spot of hair that eventually fall out. After the hair falls out a wet looking area of infection is left behind that can be highly sensitive to the horse. Catching ringworm early is important and while it can be treated at home, a mild case can quickly get worse and a vet should be called. In fact, if it is not obviously ringworm a vet may be needed to diagnose and then recommend a treatment. Ringworm tends to start on the head, but is also found in other areas that are often rubbed, like the neck, or those spots the saddle touch and moisture gather. If your horse has ringworm then hygiene is key, but hygiene is also important to prevent this from occurring. There are over the counter, human medications that will treat small areas of ringworm, including Monistat for women. This is an antifungal cream that can be applied topically, wearing gloves, to prevent the spread of ringworm.

Another common horse skin ailment is that of Rain scald, often called rain rot depending on what area you are from. Rain scald is a skin infection that happens when the skin is left wet for long periods of time. This can be from rain, humidity, or even sweat, mud, or snow. This is also common in horses with a weakened immune system as their skin breaks down much quicker. However, any horse can get rain rot. A horse with rain scald may first start showing hair loss on the back and hindquarters, but it can be found anywhere on the body. The hair can mat, fall out, and leave open sores that weep. This can be treated by the owner in most cases, but severe cases will require an antibiotic short term and this should be prescribed by the vet. To treat mild cases, use a soft brush to remove loose hair, but do not pick at any scabs. After removing the hair, wash your horse with a medicated shampoo or with straight iodine poured over the sores. After washing the horse well, and gently, make sure all excess water is removed and the horse stands to dry. Once dry, the spots can also be treated with products such as MTG or a spray animal wound care product that is useful for skin issues. Creams can be used, but sprays are usually better tolerated as the flesh can be very sensitive. This spray needs to be reapplied daily and baths should be given every few days until healed. While rain scald is not contagious, it may affect numerous horses in a barn if the problems with moisture are not addressed. The best way to prevent rain scald is to allow horses plenty of access to a clean, dry area when the weather turns. If horses are turned out in blankets, the blankets should be kept clean and dry as often as possible as damp blankets or those without air flow can create and make rain rot worse.

Mud fever can be a scary condition for horses if allowed to progress without treatment. Mud fever is contagious, but may not affect all horses in a barn. Those with weakened immune systems may not be able to fight it off as well and may suffer more over time. This is a skin condition that is typical in wet, muddy conditions. As a horse stands in mud over time the skin, especially on the legs and stomach, swells and gets scaly and red. You may be able to feel heat coming from the area which is probably sensitive to the touch. In some cases, the horse can run a fever over time that will also need treatment. You should practice taking your horse's temperature and know what is normal for your horse so it is easy to figure out if a temperature has spiked. Mud fever is actually caused by a bacterium in the mud that enters through wet skin then forms a scab and creates infection. There are preventative methods for mud fever which include access to a dry, safe, sheltered area at all times and making sure that legs and the stomach areas are cleaned well after all field work. You can wash off the legs and make sure they are dry after each muddy encounter or allow the mud to dry and use a soft brush to clean mud off. If you are in a show barn or clip your horse's legs for other reasons, then it is good to use a skin barrier cream to prevent mud fever. If your horse has mud fever it is treatable. Start by finding a clean, dry area for your horse to stay throughout the treatment, wash all affected areas with iodine or medicated shampoo, and then allow to dry completely. Finish with an antibacterial spray over all affected areas. This should be continued daily, but know hair loss is likely, so be gentle on the sensitive skin. If the infection spreads, does not heal with treatment, or a fever is noted, call the vet as mud fever left untreated can lead to death.

Cracked heels are caused by the same wet conditions as mud fever. Some horses will battle this continually, but it is treatable. As with mud fever, keep the area used for horses as clean and dry as possible by offering a dry spot to stand. If mud cannot be avoided then make sure horses are brushed often so mud is not allowed to stay on the legs and feet for long periods of time. Cracked heels can be difficult to treat because this is the part closest to the ground, just above the hoof, which is constantly moving and in contact with the elements. Treat cracked heels as you would mud fever. Additionally, keeping the hoof healthy will help keep the heel area healthier overall.

Sweet itch is a common issue for horse owners in the warmer months as insects are out and annoyingly biting. Sweet itch is an inflammation of the skin as a result of an allergic reaction to the all too common bug bites. Some horses are bothered more than others by the reaction to these bites. The horse will become itchy along its back and around the base of the tail and mane where they may rub enough to make hair fall out or be damaged. Some horses who are severely bothered will rub themselves raw trying to scratch the itch against a tree, stall, or other stationary objects. To control sweet itch, the owner should apply insect repellent regularly, but be careful that there is not a reaction to the repellant as open sores can make the horse more likely to react to strong ingredients. A veterinarian should be called to help determine a product that is safe to use as a repellant when the horse is already reacting. To keep sweet itch at bay you should allow horses to graze in drier, open areas to have less chance of contact with biting insects that are attracted to rotting plants and damp areas. There are specialized sweet itch rugs that fit over the horses poll to the tail to prevent rubbing for those with bad reactions that occur repeatedly. Sweet itch can vary from horse to horse and is not contagious, but should be treated to keep the horse healthy and happy.

Skin conditions are not the only issues a horse can have in life. Respiratory conditions for horses can be scary, but most are treatable. Some of the most common are the common cold, heaves, and a cough. Just as people, horses get colds. Colds are usually caused by a viral infection and can be contagious among horses, so any horse who is showing signs should be quarantined until better. A cold usually shows white or yellow drainage from the nose as a first sign or repeated sneezing in which the horse sprays snot. A slight temperature may be present, but not always. Glands in the throat may also be swollen. Horses get colds much like people do by sharing water troughs or food sources with other horses or being in close proximity to a sick horse at a show, in a trailer, or even in a barn. If your horse has a cold, it is important to call a vet for advice to determine the source. While treating, make sure the horse is kept warm and dry, does not share feed buckets or water sources, and is given softened food in a dust free area if there is a chance of choking. Antibiotics may be prescribed based on the type of cold your horse has and the full treatment should be given to make sure any infection has cleared up completely.

Heaves is a manageable, yet chronic, non-infectious breathing issue for horses. It is an allergic reaction to inhaled particles of dust, mold, and spores in the environment. Horses with heaves can often be ridden lightly, but the disorder will continue to worsen and weaken the horse over time. This may cut their lifespan short. Treatment involves limiting the amount of dust in the horse's environment through dust free bedding and the wetting down of hay that seems overly dusty. At some point the horse will also need medication, including steroids on a daily basis. This can get expensive over time. Some horses with heaves will lead a normal life, but others may have to have the decision made to be euthanized at some point, as breathing can become difficult and coughing almost constant. Any horse can develop heaves, but those most likely to have it are those who have been kept in poor conditions over long periods of time. It should be noted that not all dust can be avoided in a horse environment, but keeping a close eye on hay and avoiding excessive dust by keeping the barn clean is important.

Horses cough, sometimes this is innocent with a stray piece of food, but a consistent cough means there is a problem that needs treated. There are three main types of cough and until you know the origin it is best to separate the horse to prevent the spread of an infection to others. The first type of cough usually starts with an occasional cough with a runny nose which may progress to infection within a couple weeks. The other two are caused by a viral or bacterial infection that cause a cough as an allergic reaction to environmental conditions. This is why it is important to keep barns clean and well ventilated. A veterinarian should be called to determine the type of cough that is happening as it may be a symptom of something more severe. As you grow and learn as a horse owner you may recognize certain symptoms and be able to treat with what you have on hand, but this is not an option for beginners.

Other horse conditions are that are also well known are those of colic, laminitis, and cuts. Not all horses will experience these conditions, some are long term, and some are treatable. Each of these will be discussed below with possible treatments and long term outcomes.

Colic is every horse owner's worst nightmare. Colic, which some old timers will call 'tying up' can easily lead to death if unnoticed or left untreated. Many horses will colic at least once in their life time and it is highly treatable if caught early. However, colic can kill a horse within 24 hours if untreated. Colic is a term used to describe abdominal pain in a horse caused by a number of issues. There are a range of causes that include simple indigestion to a serious twisted gut that requires surgery. In all cases of colic, a veterinarian should be called and the horse should be walked continuously without food or water to prevent rolling and encourage urination and manure production. Signs of colic include a restless horse that is trying to continually roll or pawing at the ground. The pawing will be different from a horse pawing because they are bored or angry or rolling in a field to scratch an itch or enjoy the day. The horse may have elevated blood pressure, strained breathing, sweating, or repeated biting and kicking at the stomach with no cause. Some horses may also stretch out like they are trying to pee, but are unable to urinate. While waiting on the vet the horse should not be allowed to lie down or roll as this can cause the gut to become twisted. Additionally, the horse should not be allowed to eat or drink in case the colic is caused by a blockage that could be made worse. Walking allows the horse to move any food blockage around and be digested. The goal is to get the horse to poop and urinate to eliminate the pain. A vet will be able to determine the cause and offer treatment for horses with colic. Many vets will give Banamine as a treatment to make the horse pass manure which will resolve colic very quickly. In severe cases, a horse may need to have oil tube passed into the stomach through a tube in the nose to force the blockage to pass. In the case of a severely twisted gut, surgery may be recommended and will be costly. It is important to keep the horse up and moving until the colic has passed. If you have a horse prone to colic, keeping a routine and schedule will help you quickly identify if something is off and treatment needs to be sought.

Founder is a long term issue that is also known as laminitis. Founder is a common and very painful condition that effects a horse's feet, eventually pushing the bone through the hoof wall if untreated. With laminitis it is best to prevent the problem than treat it as a foundered horse can have recurring pain at any time that will turn into constant pain over time. Foundered horses are those that are overweight over long periods of time. While not all overweight horses will get laminitis, it is not worth the risk for something that can cause problems with your horsey best friend. Some horses with laminitis can still be lightly ridden, but it is best not to start with these horses if you want to ride often or compete as laminitis can flair up at any time. Horses may also require specialized shoeing for any type of riding. Early vet care is necessary as pain medication may be needed. Typical signs include rocking back and forth to keep pressure off of feet, lying down without wanting to get up, and complete lameness. While these are symptoms of laminitis, simply being lame does not necessarily mean laminitis. This is why a vet is important. An injury to a foot or heel, a cut, or even an abscess can create some of the same issues short term. Call your vet for any suspected laminitis issues and make sure to have a vet check prior to purchasing a horse to check for these issues.

A final area that may or may not require a vet is that of a cut or puncture wound. Puncture wounds should initially be treated by a vet in most cases. While waiting for the vet, do not remove the object. If it is a deep wound, try to stop the bleeding, but leaving the object is important because it may have hit something major and be holding things in place. A vet can safely remove the object. Cuts vary with horses. A simple scrape or a cut that is not deep can be treated by the owner. Clean the spot well and apply antibiotic cream. Monitor the area for heat and infection until healed. A deep cut may require a vet and stitches. Clean the area well and carefully so the vet can access and assess the cut to determine if stitches are needed. Some areas on a horse cannot be stitched, especially those over a joint, but this should be determined by a trained vet. With any severe cut, the area should be kept well cleaned and the horse not allowed to overexert themselves until healed. Cuts, bumps, and bruises will happen to any horse and horse owner. These large, usually graceful animals can be clumsy and will need help at some point to care for an injury.

Over the years this horse owner has learned to do everything from giving shots to helping drain a wound. I once had a horse go through a barbed wire fence and cut her leg down to the bone from the knee to the ankle. This horse needed immediate vet hospital care and it took over a year of daily cleaning and wrapping at home to correct the damage. I have also had to treat eye wounds, small cuts, rain rot, thrush, and heaves from home. Some of these needed vet intervention, some did not. You will learn the difference over time, just as I did. On occasion you may need to trust your gut. Two instances come to mind. One is when my mare was bred and due. The vet came out, checked her and told me to go home I had two more weeks minimum. I knew my horse well and told the vet she was wrong which made her very mad. I spend the night in the barn and was thankful I did. My mare went into labor and the baby got stuck. I had to pull him out or both would have died. My gut and my knowledge of my horse saved two lives that night. I sent pictures of our new addition to the vet the next morning, she apologized. The second instance is a horse that was given to me. It was a horse that I had ridden many years before. When he was given to me you could literally see every bone in his body. I had the vet out to give him shots and check him out. She told me to put him down on the spot. I looked into this horse's very sad eyes and told her no, that I wanted to give him a chance. This once gorgeous creature looked horrible, but within two months he was ridable again. Love can change many things. He was sold less than a year later to a family that kept him until his death. While there will come a time that you have to make the tough decision to let a horse go, sometimes they just need a chance.

If concerned it is always best to contact a vet. This is why it is important to get to know local vets and have a back-up just in case your vet is not available. If no one is available, call a local horse person for help or transport to a vet clinic or hospital if needed. Be kind to your vets and have a place that they can easily examine your horse. These are the individuals that you will call upon in the middle of the night when you are in distress. Try to stay calm and focus on the veterinarian's recommendations until they can arrive.

Choosing a Farrier, the Right Way for your Horse

If you have a horse, you will need a farrier. This is not to say that you cannot learn to trim or even shoe your own, but even if you are learning to trim it is best to have a back-up. Just as a vet should be chosen with care, your farrier will be your best friend in the horse world. Many farriers help or can offer great advice for common horse ailments, correct lameness issues with shoes, and keep your horse's feet in generally great condition. This means that your farrier should be chosen with care to make sure your new horse gets the best hoof care possible.

Farriers range in time, price, and abilities as much as trainers and veterinarians in the horse world. Before getting your first horse, inquire into local farriers where you horse will be staying. Get recommendations from current horse owners and ask what type of shoeing they get from each farrier. Some farriers are specialized in gaited horses, while others do great corrective shoeing. Some farriers will work with miniatures and ponies while other prefer not to over time. Ask about prices, availability, and whether they are kind to the horses. Many farriers are trained as farriers, but many are trained as a family legacy. Being a farrier often runs in a family as far as working with horses from the time they were very young. Do not discount on the job training over a degree or certification as many uncertified farriers are more cost effective and do a wonderful job. You may even want to inquire into their training and whether they offer other services. Some farriers will float teeth and even clean sheaths for an extra fee. Also inquire into reliability of the farrier in question. Each of these questions will help you limit your list and choose the one for you once your horse is chosen and home. Ultimately, who you choose will be dependent on your budget and what your horse needs.

Once your horse is home start trying farriers. Call a farrier of your choice and have them shoe your horse when it is due. Watch how the farrier interacts with your horse, how your horse behaves, and how well the shoes stay on. Make sure the horse is not lame after being shoed and ask the farrier if he or she notices any issues with the horse overall. If you are happy, stay with this farrier, if you are uncertain try another the next time. Within the first three months you should be able to find the farrier you like. If for some reason your farrier does not work out, then go about finding a new one in the same way. It is also a good idea to have a back-up farrier in case of emergency when your farrier is not available.

When first starting out I used the farrier that did the majority of horses at the boarding stables. He had an apprentice that helped, but I allowed the main farrier to try to shoe my horse. Unfortunately, my horse did not like this farrier and let me know. He was great with horses, very kind and gentle, but for whatever reason my horse hated him and tried to kill him each time he got near her. However, his apprentice could handle her without any issue. My horse helped me choose a farrier. So even with all the advice given in these pages, sometimes you must trust your horse knows best. That farrier stuck with me for many years, until he passed away. He took wonderful care of my first mare and the many that came after her.

Farriers do so much more than trim and shoe horses. A farrier has the amazing opportunity to see many different horses each day. This means they have seen and interacted with horses of all breeding, attitudes, and with many issues. They have been required to correct numerous foot issues over time. Your farrier is a great source of information. Do not be afraid to ask questions of your farrier as they often have techniques that may not have been considered for dealing with problem horses, beyond just shoeing. Farriers can also help you treat many minor foot issues or let you know when it is time to call a vet for an extensive exam. While not all farriers are willing to do this, many have a wealth of knowledge to share.

Though technically your farrier works for you and your horse, there are some things to do that will make his or her job easier. First, have your horse or horses caught and easy to access. Farriers are often on a schedule with many horses to do in a day, the faster they can get started, the faster they can move on to the next job. Have your horses relatively clean, especially their legs and feet. While your horse does not need to be spotless, it is nice to have clean legs and feet to work with when shoeing. If possible, have a place for your farrier to work that is, in the least, dry and well lit. Farriers work in all weathers, hot, cold, rainy, snowy, have a large stall, barn, or shelter where your horse can be tied and your farrier can work safely. Make sure your horse has a good lead rope and halter available, especially if you are not there to help your farrier. It is always best to be available when your farrier is coming, but sometimes others will have to meet them or some may be willing to work alone after getting to know your horse. Regardless of the situation, make sure you have payment read for your farrier. You would not want to provide work without pay, do not expect your farrier to do so. There are extras you can provide your farrier such as cold drinks or a fan during summer months as well as making sure to warn if your horse is sore or is a kicker as this is not someone you want to get hurt. It is okay to tip your farrier if you want, but it is not expected. Finally, if you schedule a time for your farrier to come, keep the appointment. Make sure you are ready when they arrive and that your horse is comfortable. This makes it easier for all involved. Your farrier will also be appreciative.

Picking a Horse Trainer that Fits Your Style

Trainers work in a number of ways. Some trainers give lessons in a certain discipline or with a specific breed. Some trainers break and ride horses to offer tune ups for a set price. Some trainers train only out of a specific barn and some will come to your home. A few trainers will do it all, but you need to find what works for you and your horse. This is first determined by what you want to accomplish. A trainer at a Saddlebred show barn would not be the best choice for someone who just wanted to ride trails or even run barrels. Just as a trainer who trained barrel horses is not the best option for someone who wants to learn to ride hunt seat and jump. Choose the trainer that is best for your horse, but take it further and find the trainer that works for you. This concept will be further explored below.

There are many trainers, there are also people who simply call themselves trainers. Some trainers believe in Liberty training, some believe in 'breaking' a horse, and some use a combination of methods. Some trainers are certified and some have simply lived the horseman life for many years. Trainers are men and women, young and old. Find what works for you. Additionally, trainers have different personalities and expect different levels of commitment from their riders. Some will help you become a good rider, while others will push you to be a perfect showman. Trainers often strive to build the best and strongest riders. This can be nerve racking at times, so you have to be honest with yourself about what you want to try, achieve, and how much time you are willing to put into the activity. Some trainers are soft spoken and only push as far as you are willing to go, but many will push you outside of your comfort zone to become a better rider. Some people respond well to the challenge, while others end up giving up on riding. The choice is yours and should be made carefully.

When you are choosing a trainer make sure to ask about costs and what each cost involves. If the trainer is coming to your home, then you will need a safe place to ride. You should find out ahead of time if your trainer will ride for you if there is a problem or if you want this option if it is available. Horses bond with their riders, but for new riders it can be difficult to form that bond if something is presenting a challenge. If riding at a stable you transport to or you board with then make sure you are on time for any lessons and ready to go prior to your trainer arriving. This includes grooming and saddling. Most of all, be honest with your trainer when you are comfortable and when you want to be pushed. While you should always work through fear, do not do so to the point that you no longer wish to ride. Prior to setting a lesson and time make sure to find out if you pay by the lesson, by the month, or if you are required to pay if something comes up and you must cancel the lesson. If you do need to cancel, make sure to give as much notice as possible as a trainer's time is valuable. If a particular trainer is not working out, do not be afraid to switch trainers. Leave on an amicable note so no hard feelings arise on either side.

My first trainer was not a great experience. I learned a great deal, but she was unreliable and the worst lesson she ever taught me was when I got thrown during a lesson. She made sure I was not hurt and then sent me home. I was not required to get back on and this is never good. I left to go to a new trainer shortly after and she was the polar opposite. I was required to groom, tack up, and work through issues on whichever horse I was riding for the day. Though she was tough on her students, she let us have fun. We all learned to ride bareback, clean stalls, cool down our horses, and so much more. It was not a breed specific barn so I got to be around and ride many different horses. This trainer was tough and was with me when I fell off many, many times, but she made me get back on and learn from what went wrong. I stayed with my second trainer until I moved my horses home and worked on my own. I still have contact with her over twenty years later.

Chapter 5: Basic Horse Care Needs Explained Simply

Many new horse owners do not realize the time commitment that a horse needs. Horse ownership and riding is so much more than tossing out a bucket of grain and hay or simply saddling and taking a quick ride. Those who have been in horses forever will tell you that balancing everyday life with riding and actually enjoying your horse, while still providing proper care is difficult at best. Horses are a 24 hour a day, 365 days a year commitment, one that should not be taken lightly. Even if you just do the very basics for your horse, it can be time consuming. This chapter will cover some of the basics that are necessary for you and your horse.

Feeding for Fun and Horse Nutrition

Humans have a huge variety of food choices, those with high protein, high fat, fat free, and sugar filled. Horses have almost as much variety. Ask the simple question of which horse feed is best and you will garner a million different answers. Some people swear by sweet feed, while others will tell you never to feed such an atrocity. Some will say cracked corn is a great filler, while others will say it deteriorates your horse's health. The funny part is, no one is wrong. You must get to know your horse and what you need from them in the long run.

A horse that is worked hard daily will need more calories to sustain weight and build muscle. A horse that comes to you underweight will need more calories, but this will need to occur slowly as colic can be caused by overfeeding an underweight horse. A hot horse will need feed that keeps them from being so hot, while a docile horse may need something to add a bit of pep in their step. The worst, or best part depending on your take, is that there are numerous options for every choice you need to make. This means as a horse owner you must do research and see what works best for you, your budget, and your area. Some specialty feeds are higher in cost than others, these may also be harder to obtain if you are in a small town. You may get a horse that is a picky eater that needs a certain feed, but refuses to eat it. The best thing to do is ask someone you trust to help you choose a feed. If your horse has any medical needs this should also be addressed in feeding. When first starting out, find out what your horse is used to eating and start with that type of feed. Over the course of a week or two, slowly transition your horse over with a mix that transitions to the feed of your choice. This will allow the horse and its system time to adjust.

As many feed choices are available, there are also many hay types available. Alfalfa hay is rich and many horses love it, but it is often more expensive and harder to obtain. A hay blend is much more common, though the blend may vary based on what is available in your area. When choosing your hay, make sure it has not gotten damp or wet, is not overly dusty, and does not have a moldy smell. Any one of these things can be hazardous to your horse's health. Additionally, check hay for excessive sticks, briars, or even thistle that can harm your horse by causing choking or cuts in the mouth. If a horse is stalled full time or on a dry lot, meaning no grass, then a full size horse will need between 10 and 20 pounds of hay daily. If on good grass this amount can be cut down some. A horse needs forage to help with health and digestion. Many people simply leave a round bale in a field and offer the horse free access which is fine as long as the horse does not get overweight. As with people, smaller sizes require less feed, hay, and forage.

Most horse owners will want to offer their horses treats. Most treats are safe in moderation. The occasional apple or a few carrots are never a problem. There is also an assortment of horse cookies available at most farm and feed stores. Choose treats that are low in fat and sugar to keep your equine friend healthy. In warmer months try freezing fruit in ice blocks to place in the field and allow your horse to lick the ice to get to treats. In especially warm or humid climates, try freezing the treats in Gatorade for extra electrolytes that may be lost due to sweating. Some horses enjoy peppermint candy, in moderation, or even some fruits like watermelon. Your horse may have a preference or may like any treat you offer. Though often shown in movies or shows, sugar cubes are not truly a good treat for horses. Find what works for your horse and reward them for a job well done with a special treat. Treats can also be useful for giving medication, such as mixing a pill or powder in with apple sauce or a little molasses.

Many horses will also require a few extras on top of quality hay and feed. Some horses will require supplements or will be given supplements for a specific purpose. Before adding anything to your horse's diet, check with a vet or experienced horse person so no unwanted side effects will occur. Some common extras are flax seeds or flax seed oil, black oiled sunflower seeds for dark horses to stay shiny, biotin oil or feed supplement for mane and tail growth, and even alfalfa pellets to supplement hay. Additions supplements that most horses require are access to salt and/or mineral blocks to replenish what is lost in moving around or in warm weather. These are needed even during colder months. Small salt or mineral blocks, salt on a rope, or large blocks can be purchased and placed in stalls or field. These should be kept in an area that stays relatively dry as water can cause melting. Be careful placing salt or mineral blocks with very young or baby horses as too much can make them ill. No matter which supplements you choose to give or not to give, read up on the product. Some are appropriate for horses of a certain age or workload, while others are not.

Watering Fun and Follies with your Horse

It is common sense that a horse needs access to clean, fresh water daily. What often surprises new owners is the amount of water that a single horse can drink each day. A typical size horse will need between 5 and 10 gallons of water daily. In hotter months a horse may drink up to 20 gallons of water a day. Obviously, each horse is different and may drink more or less as needed. It is important to learn your horse's drinking habits to monitor if a problem arises. A horse drinking more than normal or drinking less over time can be a sign of a health problem. Deciding how to provide horses with water is up to the owner and the situation in which the horse is kept. If stall kept, a clean, easily accessible bucket with a wide opening should be filled with clean water at least twice daily. If field kept, several clean filled buckets should be kept or a larger tub filled with water should be kept out of direct sunlight if possible. This prevents the water from getting too hot to drink and will limit algae growth. Whether using buckets or a tub, anything that holds water should be cleaned at least once a week to make sure they stay clean and bacteria growth is limited. Some stables and homes install automatic waterers that provide fresh water at all times for horses. These waterers typically have a plastic or heavy glass disc that rests on top of the opening that the horse nudges to gain access to the water. Some open pastures may have a pond or stream with plenty of water for horses, this is a great alternative, but levels and cleanliness of the water should be monitored to make sure the horse can safely drink.

Though it is important to keep hay and feed clean and dry year round, offering water to horses offers some unique challenges. If residing in a climate in which the weather gets below freezing, frozen water buckets, tanks, and lines can be a problem. There are heated water buckets and even covers available for purchase if the barn has electricity or if the horse will allow the cover to stay on the bucket. Heaters are available for plastic and metal tubs as well. These float on the water and melt ice as it forms. These are electric and must be plugged in and checked daily. These are highly functional if the horse will leave the heater in the tank. This is sometimes an issue for horses that like to pick things up. Pipes and water lines can also freeze causing a headache when it comes to hauling water to horses. It is always best to have an alternate water source or collection system available if this happens. In warmer months or in climates where drought often occurs, having a place for the horse to get cool, fresh water is just as important. A dehydrated horse can go downhill very quickly and overheating can lead to death. If you are in a drought prone area, make sure to collect rain water or have a supply of stored water for horses in case water is not readily available.

This book would be remiss if the fun aspect of water were not mentioned. Some horses love water. Most horses can naturally swim, but not all. When I was riding with friends I was with a girl taking a green broke horse for his first swim. He almost drowned before we figured out he was not being goofy; he really could not swim. Many horses will enjoy a cool hosing down after a long ride, just make sure to properly remove excess water. Some horses will enjoy playing in ponds and at the water's edge to splash and feel the mist. Some horses have even been known to play in water buckets and tubs on warm days. I owned a miniature horse who insisted on standing in the water tub on the daily basis. Look online to see some comical pictures of horses who have decided splashing in the water tank is a great pastime. This is fine and typically safe as long as the containers are horse safe and it will not get injured splashing about. A few people even set up sprinklers for their horses to play in during warmer weather. Introducing your horse to water, especially on trails or even through puddles in an arena is necessary and can be fun for horse and rider.

Learning to Groom Horses (Part of the Basics)

We have discussed feed, hay, and water, all basic parts of horse ownership, but another important part of being a good owner is bonding with your horse through grooming. Grooming offers the perfect opportunity to bond with your horse, make them look better, and check for potential health problems or injuries. Grooming is a normal and huge part of horse ownership. A horse must be groomed before riding to make sure no mud or dirt can affect the saddle or bridle. Grooming or at least a quick brushing should occur after each ride to check for injuries. Intensive grooming is necessary prior to and during any show and grooming is a special time to simply take care of your horse. When you groom a horse you have the opportunity to talk to your horse, get to know how they feel and get them used to your touch. Every part of your horse will need to be cleaned or groomed in some fashion at some point. Even if not riding, take time to groom your horses several times a week to bond and do a quick health assessment. Simply taking time to brush out a mane and tail, use a soft brush on the face and legs, and use a stiff brush or shedding blade on the body can help you get to know your horse in a way that cannot be accomplished otherwise. This will show your horse you care and allow you to learn your horse's moods, likes, dislikes, and habits.

One aspect of grooming that many new owners do not expect is that of sheath and teat cleaning. Mares, whether nursing or not, will need their teats cleaned. While this is not as intrusive as cleaning a stud or gelding, it is still necessary. Dirt, grime, and sweat builds up under a horse and they cannot reach the area to scratch or clean themselves. Take time to rinse and clean this area gently to help your horse stay comfortable. For nursing mares this area may be tender so be extra gentle and make sure to thoroughly rinse and soap that is used. For those with geldings or stallions, a more thorough cleaning is needed. At least once a year, some say more often while others say never to clean a sheath, the sheath needs cleaned. This is necessary as male horses get a buildup of smegma that can get hard and create what is called a bean. The sheath is the pocket of the male horse that holds the penis. The bean, when one is present is inside the tip of the penis and needs to be removed. The build-up is unsanitary and unhealthy for the horse. In fact, a bean can make it difficult to urinate and cause a backup if left untreated. This is not something you should try alone the first time and is something you must work up to with your horse. Some horses are not comfortable with the process and may require sedation by the veterinarian in order to be cleaned. Many people prefer to let the vet take care of the cleaning yearly. If you are interested in methods used to complete sheath cleaning, numerous videos exist online to offer you options. Though this is often considered a 'gross' job, it is one that is needed for your horse's overall health. On a comical note, having a non-horse person help you clean a sheath is always funny, but prepare them for the smell as it is indescribably bad on many horses.

Seasonal Concerns Every Horse Owner Should Know

Most aspects of horse care have been well covered or at least touched upon in previous chapters, but there are a few seasonal concerns that are noteworthy. As mentioned, many problems occur in the colder, winter months. Frozen water buckets, tanks, and lines are the most common issue. While having an extra supply of water is great, it is not always feasible due to storage limitations. Heaters and bucket cozies are also wonderful, but can also fail. This means that the layers of ice that have formed need to be broken, sometimes daily. A hammer or ice pick is always handy for larger tanks, but for regular five gallon buckets it is often easiest to simply turn them upside down and stomp on the bottom. This will loosen the ice that will typically slide out. If buckets will not break open it is best to have spares so the frozen buckets can be moved to a heated area to melt. This writer has been known to bring completely frozen buckets into the house to turn upside down and shower with hot water. The buckets break open, but you will end up with feed and hay in your shower. While horses can handle the cold well, they still need a dry shelter that blocks the wind year round. If you choose to blanket your horse during cooler months, then make sure the blanket is breathable and that it gets cleaned regularly. Other concerns in colder months with poor conditions is that of footing. Ice and snow is not usually a problem for horses, but icy patches can make leading horses treacherous if not aware. Make sure to wear boots with traction to give yourself a better chance at staying upright.

Spring and summer months, when it starts to warm up, can also bring on challenges with horses. The most common is the battle with insects beginning. Fleas, gnats, horse flies, and many other biting insects emerge and begin to attack. Purchase a fly spray, fly traps, and even hang barn safe fans to keep your horses happy and limit the number of bites acquired. After the horse has been out or on a trail ride, check and remove any ticks that may have found their way onto your horse. Spring also means shedding season. This means that your horse will begin losing its winter coat and you will be covered in hair for at least three months. For women this means you will have horse hair down your bra and in places you never want to find horse hair. For anyone who grooms, this means you will sneeze horse hair and dust for weeks on end, but it is a sign that spring has arrived. A good shedding blade is important for your horse and your own comfort. Extra water will be needed in warmer months and monitoring how quickly your horse moves to grass, if that is an option, is something that must be done.

Horses are truly a year round job. Each day offers victories and challenges. Take each moment of the day as it comes, stay calm, and learn from your horse victories and failures. You will learn lessons about yourself, your limits, and your abilities. You will also learn to improvise as horses have a way of creating new issues all the time. The good news is, it is worth all the time, effort, and money as you bond with your new best friend.

Chapter 6: Commitments of Horse Ownership: A Reality Check

This book in its entirety has touched on the commitments of owning a horse. As most horse owners do not stick with only one horse for very long, the time commitments tend to grow as well. Even if you only have one horse, the amount of time needed to keep your horse happy and healthy can be overwhelming. If you have read this far, hopefully you are taking all this into consideration and thinking practically about ownership and housing your horse. While a boarding stable will take some of the work out of horsemanship, there is a bigger financial commitment and a time commitment. Read on to learn about further time commitments that may have been overlooked.

Scheduling and Time Commitments of Horse Ownership

If you keep your horse at home then you set the schedule, but boarded horses stay on the schedule of the stable owner or workers. Either one is fine as long as feed time and routine is relatively consistent. Horses like routine, but even though your horse may complain, serving a meal a few minutes late is not the end of the world. Having a routine you can stick to with your horse not only allows them to know what is happening, but allows you to quickly catch any odd behaviors that may signify a problem. Usually, at least in colder months or at times when grass is not available, horses are fed twice a day. A morning feeding with hay or turnout and offering fresh water is typical and then the same is offered in the evening with horses brought indoors. This can be altered to fit your needs, but if feeding twice in a day the feedings do need to be separated by at least 8 to 10 hours so the horse has time to digest. If keeping a horse at home then there should also be time to clean stalls, clean any buckets or tanks that need it, and time to spend grooming and riding. It can be hard to get used to adding all of this to your schedule and this should be taken into consideration. Most horse owners will tell you that if you plan to spend an hour at the barn, you will probably spend two minimum. The hard work will pay off as you will have a best friend for life.

If you board, a great deal of this basic feeding, stall cleaning, and offering hay or turnout will probably be taken care of for you, but this does come at a cost. You will also need to make time to drive to the boarding or riding stable to spend time with your horse. One situation is not necessarily better than the other, but each have different levels of time that will need committed to your horse. For the remainder of this section the focus will be on taking care of your horse at home as more of a time commitment is needed.

If keeping your horse at home, you are required to offer constant care. If you are also working or have a family this can be difficult, but must be added to your routine. Teaching children to help will not only instill a work ethic, but help them to respect animals and possibly catch the horse bug, making horsemanship a family activity. Make sure if you are involving children that you teach proper safety and care methods so injury is less likely. It will take you awhile to figure out a schedule and some days will be easier than others. One time and scheduling issues that new owners tend to forget is that of needing to go out of town or schedule a vacation. This writer has not taken a vacation in many years. Even overnight trips must be planned around the horses. Those who have horses, rarely vacation, unless the horse goes with them. If you do need to be out of town, care for your horses will need to be arranged. This can be scary as too much change for a horse can create health problems. You will need a trusted friend or pet sitter that understands your horses needs and can fit into your schedule. Finding this person can take time and effort, so find several that can help just in case. Also keep in mind that your perfectly healthy horse will seemingly find a way to get hurt or sick each time you plan a trip, leave someone in charge who knows how to handle the situation.

Other time commitments that people tend to forget or overlook are things like buying, moving, and storing hay and feed for horses, dealing with bad weather, and scheduling with vets, farriers, and if needed other horse related professionals. No matter what the weather, tornadoes, snow, rain, or 100-degree heat, your horse still needs your care. This can be exhausting at times, but it is a necessary part of ownership. You will need extra time to purchase and haul hay and feed, as well as extra time and effort to store it. This will all be added expenses to your budget, so plan accordingly. None of this information is designed to scare potential owners, but a horse is a big commitment in many ways that should be considered before bringing the magnificent animal into your life.

Financial Planning for Adding to your Horse Herd

As mentioned, few horse owners stay with only one horse long term. Horses are herd animals and do better with a friend, but a friend means more of a time and financial commitment for the owner. Having more than one horse means buying more feed, hay, providing a larger or extended shelter, needing more room, and twice the vet and farrier bills. You must also find time to care for multiple horses, to ride and groom. Many people do not find this a problem, but realistically look over your personal finances to make sure you can offer long term homes to your horses with proper care. Many people accidently become collectors of horses without expecting the financial strain that is attached. If finding another horse friend is not in the cards, but you do not want your horse to be alone, many have found that goats, donkeys, sheep, or even chickens, offer interaction for their horses that is sufficient. You will also be your horse's best friend and trusted human once a bond is formed.

As a horse owner it is important to plan ahead and have a contingency plan and emergency fund. One injury, one piece of broken equipment, or a failing vehicle can get costly very quickly. If you have an emergency fund, then these issues are not as much of a problem. The one thing you must remember, whether you have a single horse or a whole herd, is that they will require sacrifice of your funds, time, and at times body and sanity. However, all the time, money, and sacrifice will be worth it because your horse will teach you lessons in life and love that you cannot even imagine.

Chapter 7: Horse Owner Advice to Beginners that No One Shares

Thank you for taking time to read this guide. Hopefully you have made a decision to buy a first horse, add to your herd, or simply learned what is necessary for horse ownership. There are many topics that were barely touched upon and several that require an entire novel of their own. This final section is not based on fact, it is opinion and wisdom from those that have been there and done that with horses. Some of these words are true, some are funny, and some are just common sense, but they are all things every beginner needs to hear in order to become a strong, sound horse owner.

Words of Wisdom

- Every horse, just as every rider, has a different personality. Choose wisely.
- You will fall off; you will get thrown. Many feel that until you have 'brought some dirt' at least three times, you are not a real rider.
- Horses are smart, caring animals that do not know their size or yours, behave accordingly.
- A horse will get himself around a tree, but does not account for your knees around the same tree.
- When buying remember: One white foot, buy a horse: Two white feet, try a horse: Three white

feet, look well about them: Four white feet, do well without them. This is an old saying with a few variations that has been around for many years.

- The calmest horse in the barn will be the one that surprises you the most when it decides to act up.
- No matter how many times you cross the same puddle, see the same bag, or walk past the same building, those items will at some time spook your horse.
- The swirls and whirls on a horse's head can indicate personality. This is based in science and specifics can be found online.
- Mares have a mare stare that can be highly intimidating.
- Chestnut mares are the meanest horses ever created according to those in the horse world. This has weirdly been my experience as well.
- The smaller the horse, the bigger the brat. Miniature horses are said to be created by the devil.
- If you build a better stall, lock, or room, a better, more determined horse will find a way in or out.
- A bath almost assures your horse will roll, especially if it is white or you need him or her to be clean.
- Blue-eyed horses are insane. There is no proof of this, but it is something many believe. However, blue-eyed horses can be more prone to eye and sight issues.
- If you think your horse is perfectly safe and will not get hurt, he or she will find a way. Be prepared.

- Human items can be used on horses, just get creative.
- Always, ALWAYS, carry an extra halter and lead rope.
- You can break a horse by breaking its spirit, but you are better off allowing the horse to learn and grow with you in a mutual friendship.
- Learn to drive and back a trailer before you need to.
- Bleach, peroxide, Dawn, vinegar, and iodine will be your best friends.
- Your body will probably give out before your horse. Stay positive, any time spent with horses, riding or not, is worth it.
- Choose your boarding barn, trainer, and horse wisely.
- Grade horses are just as good as papered horses as far as riding.
- Buy in the winter, shaggy horses cost less on purchase.
- Be firm, not abusive with your horse.
- Have a strong fence.
- When buying, get videos, have the owner wait to catch the horse, and watch it being saddled.
- Never take a horse trailer to look at a horse the first time.
- Visit your horse every day, even if he or she isn't kept at home.
- Never corner a scared horse, you can be seriously hurt if you are seen as a threat.
- Learn to listen to your horse, they speak with small actions. The flick of an ear or swish of a tail can speak volumes.

- People do not have horse problems, horses have people problems.
- Ask for help when needed.
- Most of all, advice is free and everyone has some. Take advice with a grain of salt and find what works for you and your horse.

When I got my first horse I was young. My father bought a horse that was headed to an auction. I did not find her particularly beautiful and she was far too much horse for me in the beginning. However, I learned more from that mare than any other horse after her. I had her for 18 years and held her as she died. That horse, her name was Ricky's Firefly, taught me how to be a good, patient, and caring person. She saved my life many times over. I would not trade those years, those falls, those failures, and those victories for anything in the world. Over the years, through the horses, I received copious amounts of advice. Some advice was taken, some immediately forgotten. Always be open to what people tell you, but use only what works for you and your horse. I was told for years that my horse was not built for what I used her for, but she excelled. I was once told I could not ride a trail class in an English saddle, I beat the guy that told me that and he got very angry, contesting the win. I happily offered him my ribbon though the judge upheld the win, as the feeling of accomplishment was much better. Everyone has an opinion, even me in writing this book, but you have to make the choices that are best for your horse and yourself. Even if you make the wrong choice, learn from it and keep moving forward.

About the Expert

Author Amanda Wills started riding horses when she was 13 years old and had her first registered Quarter horse by the age of 14. The chestnut nightmare that was then hers was the most imperfect horse a beginner could ask for in life, but the mare was hers. Together they learned from very difficult lessons in respect, riding, showing, and life. Amanda credits the mare, named Molly, with getting her through some very difficult teenage years. Molly stayed with her until she died at the age of 26. Throughout the years, Amanda had several other horses, rode for others, and even worked as a groom. The numerous people she had the blessed opportunity to get to know have offered words of caution and wisdom over the years. Most of these words were from highly experienced horse men and women and have been shared in the pages of this book. Hopefully you will gain and knowledge and inspiration from what is shared.

HowExpert publishes quick 'how to' guides on all topics from A to Z by everyday experts. Visit HowExpert.com to learn more.

Recommended Resources

- HowExpert.com – Quick 'How To' Guides on All Topics from A to Z by Everyday Experts.
- HowExpert.com/free – Free HowExpert Email Newsletter.
- HowExpert.com/books – HowExpert Books
- HowExpert.com/courses – HowExpert Courses
- HowExpert.com/clothing – HowExpert Clothing
- HowExpert.com/membership – HowExpert Membership Site
- HowExpert.com/affiliates – HowExpert Affiliate Program
- HowExpert.com/writers – Write About Your #1 Passion/Knowledge/Expertise & Become a HowExpert Author.
- HowExpert.com/resources – Additional HowExpert Recommended Resources
- YouTube.com/HowExpert – Subscribe to HowExpert YouTube.
- Instagram.com/HowExpert – Follow HowExpert on Instagram.
- Facebook.com/HowExpert – Follow HowExpert on Facebook.